Awakening the BlueLotus:
A Reiki Level One Handbook

By Storm Faerywolf

©2010-2011 Storm Faerywolf. All rights reserved. No part of this book may be reproduced or transmitted in any form or by any means, electronic or mechanical, including photocopying, recording or by any information storage and retrieval system, without written permission from the author, except for the inclusion of brief quotations in a review.

This book is designed to provide information on using Reiki, from the perspective of the BlueLotus school. It is presented with the understanding that the publisher and author are not licensed medical or psychological doctors and are not engaged in offering medical, psychological or legal services and do not prescribe the use of any technique for treatment of medical or psychological problems without the advice of a licensed medical or psychological practitioner. Reiki is *not* a substitute for qualified medical or psychological care.

The intent of the author is to offer information of a general nature to assist in the search for spiritual well being and development. The author and publisher assume no responsibility for any loss or damage caused, or alleged to have been caused, directly or indirectly, by the information contained in this book. If these terms are unacceptable then please do not use the information in this book.

"The Reiki Principles
The Secret Method of Inviting Blessings
The spiritual Medicine of Many Illnesses...
For today only anger not, worry not...
Be Grateful and humble, do your work with appreciation.
Be kind to all.
In the morning and at night, with hands held in prayer,
Think this in your mind; chant this with your mouth.
The Usui Reiki Method to change your mind and body for the better."

-Mikao Usui

Preface

This book is based on my Reiki Level One class and is intended first and foremost to be a supplement to the teachings given therein. Since Reiki is not passed as ordinary knowledge and instead as an energetic event, one cannot simply pick up this manual and become a Reiki practitioner. For this, one must be attuned (aka initiated) by a qualified Reiki Master/Teacher.

One can, however, learn some of the history of our tradition, as well as some meditative and energetic exercises that will enhance their experiential understanding of energy and at the very least prepare them for practicing Reiki should they eventually become attuned to our path.

BlueLotus *is the name that I have given to my practice and school of Reiki. In Eastern thought the lotus represents regeneration and spiritual illumination. It is also a symbol of the ability to transcend the muck (where it is rooted) and grow even though the dirtiest of waters (life experience) and into the pure sunlight of enlightenment (where the flower blooms). The blue lotus also represents wisdom, and to the ancient Egyptians symbolized rebirth, as they saw it close and descend beneath the waters each night, only rise up from the waters the following day. To me this is a perfect symbol for Reiki practice; a practice that promotes enlightenment, wisdom, transformation, and renewal.*

At the end of this book is a list of resources that you may find helpful in your search. I've included suggestions of music appropriate for use in Reiki sessions, as well as recommended additional reading.

TABLE OF CONTENTS

INTRODUCTION 9
CHAPTER ONE, "What is Reiki?" 17
CHAPTER TWO: "History of Reiki" 21
CHAPTER THREE: "Philosophy" 35
CHAPTER FOUR: "Practice" 49
CHAPTER FIVE: "Ethics & Legality" 71
CHAPTER SIX: "The Attunement" 73
CHAPTER SEVEN: "Lineage" 77
CHAPTER EIGHT: "Conclusion & Resources" 79

INTRODUCTION

My first introduction to Reiki was in the form of a discussion with one of my first spiritual teachers back in the late 1980's. She explained to me how healing energy was channeled through the hands of the practitioner and into the recipient, adding that it "could do no harm". I was fascinated by the knowledge that the energy was passed by way of a controlled metaphysical experience in which specific symbols were used in order to "unlock" this healing potential from within. Because my teacher was *not* a Reiki teacher (and because the fees associated with Reiki classes at that time were so prohibitive, especially for a teenager) I was not able to learn this modality at the time, and settled for using other psychic healing methods that I was able to cultivate on my own.

Years passed, and I was perfectly happy in my own spiritual and healing practice. I would often hear about Reiki, but again the costs were a barrier. One day in May 1996, a Reiki teacher was scheduled to give an introductory class at the metaphysical shop where I worked. She set-up her materials in preparation for the class, but no one came. Feeling badly (and sensing that perhaps this was my opportunity) I decided to bite the bullet and pay the $100.

When the class began I became doubtful of her information, as she explained quite matter-of-factly that this was the healing method that Jesus performed, citing her beliefs as fact that he travelled to India in the infamous "lost years" and learned this ancient technique from the sages there. She also referenced an Atlantian connection, as well as cited Native American spirituality. I felt that I had fallen prey to another New Age scam; perhaps not intentional on her part, but one that purported to be something even though the evidence proved otherwise. I was disappointed.

As if to underscore my newly formed negative opinion, when it came time for her to pass the attunement, she was concerned that I was wearing a black shirt, saying that "Reiki has trouble going through black" (a charge that I have never heard before or since). I needed to remove my shirt for the attunement to work. (This from a spiritual system that purports to be able to send the energy without regard to space or time.) I internally rolled my eyes in judgment, convinced that this woman was nothing more than a flake if she believed in what she was saying, or a charlatan if she didn't. I gave her the benefit of the doubt and decided to secretly judge her as well-intentioned but sadly misinformed.

Shirtless, I sat in preparation for the attunement, resigning myself to the experience which I assumed would be nothing more than an opportunity to close my eyes and contemplate my navel.

With my hands held in prayer, my eyes closed, I began to relax as she began her breathing exercises and placed her hands on my head. I began to drift, as she focused her breath on my crown and send energy (I could feel it!) into my head and neck... I was floating... blissful. Everything after that was a sweet blur; when it was finished I opened my eyes and everything seemed *different*. I could not (and can not) explain exactly *how*... I just felt... better. Happy. Relaxed. Content. I realized that my judgment was premature; her information might not have been the best, but the *energy*... What had transpired was a genuine energetic experience and no one was more surprised than I.

That night I forgot to do many things that are normally done to close the store (luckily I remembered to put the money away and lock the door!) and that feeling remained, although lessened, for several days after. I continued my own healing practice, now coupled with a few simple exercises and specific hand positions that were part of the instruction, and I noticed that while I didn't feel that I was plugged into any different energy than what I had been accustomed to before, I *did* feel as if things just flowed more clearly; the energy seemed more *available* as if it was just a hair's breadth away from flowing through me, something that I had *not* experienced before. I also seemed to be able to channel *more* energy than I had previously, so regardless of the fact that the energy itself wasn't new, I felt that the whole "experiment" was a successful one.

About a year later I received my second level attunement from a friend. It felt different that time; less "blissful", more manageable. At first it caused me to question whether or not anything had actually transpired, but again the proof was in the pudding; once more I felt "cleared" of obstacles that were preventing me from channeling more of the energy, and indeed it did feel as if my channel was again widened; the energy felt stronger when I actually went to use it. Again, a successful endeavor.

It was here also, however, that I decided to stop doing Reiki as a specific practice. Part of my decision was based in the fact that one of the symbols that I had been taught was very *complicated*. A Japanese kanji with 22 strokes in its making was not something that my brain felt it could memorize and so in classic sour grapes fashion, I decided that it wasn't for me. And promptly discontinued working with the symbols and the traditional aspects of the work.

I did, however, continue to use what else I had been taught. The energy still felt clear and available, and the more I worked with it the less "specifically Reiki" it became. If it was all about plugging into and using "universal life-energy" then it seemed silly to classify the energy itself as specifically "Reiki" when I was using the energy practice for purposes other than what I had been taught, such as working with crystals or empowering herbs and candles. I decided that Reiki II was enough for me, and so that's where I stayed for many years.

Besides Reiki I am a practitioner of many other spiritual and magical paths, most notably the F(a)eri(e) tradition of witchcraft, which is a sorcerous path of soul development. In this system, working with energy is paramount, and I found that my previous training in Reiki was quite helpful in keeping things clear and strong for this work. As a teacher in that tradition I found myself teaching someone who wanted to exchange Reiki attunements for her classes and so I agreed thinking that at least I could "finish what I had started" so many years ago, even though I had no intention of teaching Reiki or even practicing it professionally. During the course of her training with me I received the Reiki I and II attunements, and then she promptly left the country for India to pursue another spiritual path there. I was destined, it seemed to remain at the second level. Just as well, as I still had no intention to teach.

A couple of years later my husband and I bought a metaphysical store in Walnut Creek, an affluent suburb in the San Francisco East Bay Area. Renamed *The Mystic Dream*, we saw it as an opportunity to connect many divergent spiritual paths to better serve the community and to allow our own spiritual practices to grow and evolve. It was shortly after taking over the shop that I began to have the dreams.

They happened every night for months and they were always the same: I was in a non-descript place and an older woman or gentleman would be showing me how to draw a symbol with the palm of their hand. It would appear over me as if painted by a calligrapher's brush and then melt into me. Then I was asked to "paint" the symbol in the same way. I had never (consciously) seen the symbol before, but in the dream (and upon waking) I just *knew* that this symbol was connected to

Reiki. I would arise in the morning and my hands would be buzzing, a common experience reported by Reiki practitioners. I felt *the calling*. I now was ready to take my practice of Reiki "to the next level"; I was ready to pursue Mastership.

Since I had previously scoffed at my ability to learn the complicated third symbol, I decided that I needed to immerse myself in it completely, but my notes from my Reiki II attunement were nowhere to be found. How could I learn the symbol without my notes?! I bought a copy of Diane Stein's *Essential Reiki* which published many Reiki symbols (and caused quite a stir in the Reiki community because of it). I found the symbol in question, and began to practice, practice, practice, until I had it memorized. I worked with it energetically and it was immediately *available*; it was as if no time had passed at all. I was ready to take the next step.

I began to search for someone who was teaching the Master level and what I found was both confusing and amazing. When doing an internet search I learned that some Reiki Masters were offering attunements via long distance, something that I had not considered before. Once such person offered to do it for $20 and when I mentioned my lack of certificate for Reiki II I was told that I wouldn't even need to have received the first or second attunements; he would just do the Master attunement for me regardless. I was intrigued, but also felt that the intimacy that is present when performing such a rite in-person was necessary for me, not to mention that I felt that I really wanted to *earn* it; to simply give me the attunement sight-unseen without regard to what work I had done before, smacked as a disrespect to the overall tradition, and so I decided to look elsewhere.

In my neo-Pagan community I met a man named Eddy Gutierrez who in addition to his work in various tribal and neo-Pagan traditions was also a Reiki Master. We had been fans of each other's work in the context of Paganism but had only recently met at Pantheacon, a large convention for neo-Pagan practitioners in the Bay Area. I approached him and he said that he did not generally pass the Master/Teacher level as Reiki II was all most people needed to do Reiki professionally. He also said that his practice was closer to what might be seen as Japanese in that it was the practice that determined the Master and not one's ability to pay for an attunement. He was open to visiting us to see if our practice and ability was sufficient to warrant the title. "If you are living as a Reiki Master then I will confirm and attune you as a Master."

We spent a weekend together and practiced our various paths... magic, mediation, and of course Reiki. He tested us on the symbols, on our philosophies of how Reiki worked. He asked us what we knew of its history, and most importantly, he asked for demonstrations of our ability to channel Reiki in a session. Satisfied of our knowledge and ability he passed us the Reiki III attunements and certified us as Reiki Master/Teachers.

After the attunements, Eddy explained that our Reiki lineage was dual; since many practitioners have had additional instruction and attunements to various other symbols and practices it is not an uncommon experience. Someone in our "up-line" had been "re-attuned" so as to have access to these additional symbols which purport to have originated in Tibet. Eddy then instructed us in the use of the Master symbols, one of which was this Tibetan symbol, and "just happened" to be that mysterious symbol that I had been dreaming about. If I had needed confirmation that this was the right person to have chosen to complete my training, it was here in this revelation. I had the dream once more that night. And then they stopped. Moved from my sub-conscious to my conscious mind, the symbol was inside me and so the dreams weren't needed anymore.

I have found great joy in practicing and teaching Reiki. I love being able to provide a student with "just that little piece" that enables their own spiritual practice to grow in new and unexpected ways. It has also informed my own overall practice and all the myriad of things that I do. It is with great pleasure that I offer this handbook for the first level of Reiki practice. May it help you along your path.

CHAPTER 1: What is Reiki?

Reiki is a traditional spiritual energy practice that originated in Japan and promotes balance and healing. It is an excellent method for reducing stress, enhancing meditation, spiritual & psychic development, as well as being a compliment to more orthodox medicine. Reiki is generally administered to oneself or others by laying on of hands, but may also be performed via long distance. Unlike most other types of spiritual and energetic healing, Reiki does not deplete the life-force of the user, and leaves both the practitioner and recipient balanced and energized.

Reiki works by way of channeling spiritual energy through the practitioner and into the body of the recipient in order to restore energetic balance. The basic premise behind energy healing is that physical disease is the cause of energetic imbalances in the subtle bodies. Once those imbalances are addressed then healing can occur.

In the West Reiki often gets translated as "Universal Life-force Energy". This is not entirely correct as it fails to take into account the nuances that are present in the Japanese language. The Japanese word "Reiki" (pronounced "ray-key") is a compound of the words "Rei" (meaning "soul", "spiritual power", and "divine wisdom") and "Ki" (like the Chinese "Chi" or "Qi", meaning "life-force" or "energy").

Modern kanji characters for "Rei" and "Ki"

Traditional (pre-1940) kanji characters for "Reiki"

More correctly, when taken together we can understand Reiki to mean "spiritually guided life-force", or in other words it is universal life-force energy that is guided by a higher spiritual (divine) wisdom. This higher guidance is an important aspect of Reiki that we shall explore in depth later in this book. In Japan the word Reiki can refer to any number of energetic spiritual practices while in the West the word applies specifically to the traditional method of spiritual healing that we are concerned with here.

Reiki is an initiatory tradition, meaning that practitioners must undergo a metaphysical or spiritual initiation in order to become channels for the energy. These initiations are commonly referred to as "attunements". This is a ceremony in which specific symbols common to Reiki are ceremonially placed into the energy-body or "aura" of the initiate by a Reiki Master/Teacher.

There are commonly three levels in Reiki. Level One (Shoden) is an introduction to the energy. This attunement clears away blocks or obstacles that may be present and widens ones channel for life-force. Primarily Level One is concerned with the art of self-healing, but it is not uncommon (and is even encouraged) that Level One practitioners engage in practicing their skills on others. Some refer to this as the "Physical Healing level", though this gives the false impression that the healings received at this level are purely physical. While symbols are energetically passed as part of this attunement, they are not taught or explained to the student, as the focus of Reiki I is to get to know the energy and the mental contemplation of symbols can often prove to be a distraction from that introductory process.

Level Two (Okuden) widens the channel further and grants energetic access to –and instruction on the use of –additional symbols that allow the practitioner to do specific things with the energy, most notably work with mental & emotional healing, as well as to send Reiki over long distance. This is sometimes referred to as the "Mental/Emotional Healing level". For most individuals who wish to pursue Reiki professionally, Reiki II is all that is necessary.

Level Three (Shinpiden) is the Master (or Master/Teacher) level in which even more symbols are given which enable the practitioner to work with issues that are spiritual in nature (and sometimes called the "Spiritual Healing level"), as well as grant the ability to pass attunements to all levels of Reiki. This level is generally reserved for those individuals who have mastered the previous work and material and who feel a calling to work spiritually and to teach. In *BlueLotus* a written test is part of the application process to be considered for this level.

There are some lineages of Reiki that have a "fourth level" which is the result of breaking Level Three into two separate levels, each with their own attunement. Sometimes referred to as Reiki III and Reiki IV, or Reiki IIIa and Reiki IIIb, this separates the level of Reiki Master into Master/Practitioner and Master/Teacher. This represents a change in the tradition of Reiki from the original Three degree system.

There are two possible reasons for this change as far as I can see. One is that there may have been a Reiki II student who felt that they were called to work with issues of a spiritual nature, but were *not* called to teach; their Reiki Master then augmenting the Reiki master attunement to grant this ability while not passing the energetic ability to pass attunements to others. The other possibility is that someone along the line decided that it was more profitable to insert another level before Reiki Master/Teacher. However this practice may have begun, there are now many practitioners of Reiki who were initiated/attuned with this practice and so to them this is traditional. *BlueLotus* adheres to the original three degree system.

Originally the symbols passed in Reiki attunements were closely guarded secrets, never to be revealed to those not attuned to the second level. While some modern practitioners still adhere to this secrecy, many do not and examples and descriptions of the Reiki symbols (as well as numerous additional newer symbols) can be found published in books, carved on crystals and stones, on candles, statues, wands, and even on the internet. *BlueLotus* does not concern itself with any decisions that its practitioners make regarding this issue; it is assumed that the individual will make whatever choices are right for them as the situation warrants.

CHAPTER 2: History of Reiki

There are now many different "histories" of Reiki that are commonly accepted by many of its practitioners. This is because until relatively recently information about Reiki was only passed orally, leaving the information subject to corruption through poor memory, laziness, fantasy, or even blatant misinformation. Among these "mythical histories" of Reiki are stories of how the founder was a Christian missionary or monk, or that he "rediscovered" Reiki which is then usually attributed to something older and more exotic (such as India, Egypt, or Tibet) or even otherworldly (such as Atlantis or UFOs). While these stories are colorful and might even have some poetic value as "teaching stories" actual research into the origin of Reiki and the life of its founder have proven them to be little more than revisionist history. Now that we have access to real information, let us celebrate the true origins of Reiki, and the life of the man who founded it.

Mikao Usui
1865-1926

The tradition that has come to be known in the West as Reiki was founded by a gentleman by the name of Mikao Usui. He was born on August 15, 1865, in the village of Taniai, which is now located near present day Nagoyo.[1] Usui studied several spiritual systems during his life, most notably Buddhism in which he became a lay Tendai priest. He was heavily influenced by Shintoism and was even known to practice Shugenja (a form of shamanism that combines elements of Shinto and Buddhist practices)

---

[1] Rand, William L (2005). *Reiki the Healing Touch: First and Second Degree Manual*. Michigan, USA: Vision Publications. p. I-13. ISBN 1886785031.

and to employ *jumon*; spells and incantations derived from Shinto and Taoism.

During his varied studies he was exposed to many different meditational and healing practices, most notably Kikou, a Japanese form of Qi Gong. Like its Chinese counterpart, Kikou involves the practitioner engaging in rigorous internal energy exercises and a series of active and restful poses in order to build of a charge of "ki"; life-force energy. When a sufficient charge has been built, it is then discharged into the recipient by way of channeling it through the hands over them. While this can prove to be effective it also often leaves the healer tired and depleted.

Usui began to hear stories about ancient healers and mystics who employed techniques of spiritual healing that did *not* deplete the life-force of the practitioner, but he could find no descriptions of what these practices actually were. He became fascinated with these stories and set out to find out the truth about these ancient practices.

In March of 1922, after having spent years pursuing the secrets of the elusive healing technique, Usui travelled to Mt. Kurama, a sacred site and place of worship north of Kyoto, to meditate and fast for 21 days with the intent to find this ancient healing practice. As the story is told, he gathered by him 21 stones and at the end of each day he would throw one of them away to mark the time spent on his quest.

At dawn of the last day, just as he was beginning to despair, he saw a great ball of light approaching him. He became fearful but thinking that perhaps this was the answer to his prayers did not move, though his first instinct was to turn and run away. The light began to approach faster and finally hit him between the eyes or on the top of his head. He fell to the ground and perceived millions of "bubbles of light" of all different sizes and colors of the rainbow, some of which contained golden symbols that he recognized from his previous studies but had failed to understand their significance until that moment.

After experiencing the revelation, Usui felt energized and in full possession of the knowledge of the healing technique that he had sought. Though he had fasted for nearly a month he felt strong and stable. This is considered to be the first of the four (or, in some versions of the story, three) miracles. Elated, he began to run down the mountain and stubbed his big toe on a rock, injuring his toe and dislodging the nail. Instinctively he placed his hands on the injured toe and the pain began to subside. He held it until he felt no more pain and was delighted to find that it had completely healed. This is the second miracle.

At or near the base of the mountain he saw an inn (in some accounts this is a Zen Buddhist monastery) and decided to eat. He was warned against eating too much after having just spent so much time fasting, but with his new found vigor he disregarded the advice and proceeded to indulge. Though he ate great amounts of food immediately after a prolonged fast he suffered no ill effects. This is the third miracle.

While there he noticed the daughter of the innkeeper who was suffering with a terrible toothache; her face swollen, and in tremendous pain. Usui placed his hands upon her face and she was healed. This is the fourth miracle.

Usui began to share this healing technique with those in need, working in the poorest parts of the country offering healing to all who requested it. When the great earthquake struck the following year he found himself thrust into a mélange of desperation and opportunity; over 144,000 reported dead and even more wounded meant wide-spread disease and depression, but Usui rose to the challenge and began to share Reiki on a wider scale, working mostly for free. Because he worked tirelessly in the "beggar's quarters" with those who needed it most, word began to spread about Usui's Healing Method. The elders were pleased because it represented a return to the older values of spiritual development, while people of a more modern sensibility were curious and excited because of the seemingly miraculous healings that were taking place.

As he continued to work, giving healings for free it is said that he began to notice that some of those who had previously been healed were returning to their unhealthy ways. Because of this Usui realized that the individual must be emotionally and intellectually invested in their own healing, and so he decided that the best way to achieve this was to charge a fee for his services. In this a person who paid money for a session would be less likely to simply return to unhealthy behaviors if they knew that they would again be expected to make payment. The idea is that those who receive something for free, do not value it. Whether or not this story is true is unclear, but it (and the psychology behind it) is cited as the reason that most practitioners of Reiki charge for their services.

His services were in such high demand that he decided to open a clinic and begin teaching Reiki as well as offering healings. His clinic was named "Usui Reiki Ryoho Gakkai" which means, "Society of the Usui Spiritual Energy Healing Method". His approach was far more intuitive than how most Westerners practice today. Instead of the attunement method that is commonly used today, Usui-sensei used a process called *reiju* which was common in Tendai Buddhism. Reiju is a type of informal energetic blessing. Students who had gathered in his school, after receiving instruction and engaging in practice, would receive reiju which would, over time, act much as the Reiki attunements do today; widening the energetic channels and clearing away blocks that may prevent one from channeling the energy.

One of Usui's students, Chujiro Hayashi, is credited with formalizing the (lengthy, informal) reiju process into the attunement forms that we are familiar with today. What once took weeks or months could now be achieved in the span of a few days, or even a few minutes. Originally the Level One attunement consisted of four separate attunements, but most lineages now perform just one attunement for each level. (One idea that has been proposed is that the original four were symbolic of the many reiju "mini attunements" that were passed by Usui and their number may be derived from the "four miracles" that Usui performed when Reiki was revealed to him. Because this was purely symbolic many lineages have abandoned the four-part Level One attunement in favor of the more streamlined single attunement.)

Chujiro Hayashi
1879-1940

Hayashi met Usui in 1925 and studied with him for only 10 months before Usui's death in 1926 from a stroke. After the death of Usui, Hayashi took over his master's clinic and renamed it *Hayashi Reiki Kenkyu-kai*, or "Hayashi Reiki Research Society" to reflect the significant changes that he made to the overall system.

Some accounts have indicated that Hayashi was asked to leave, causing him to open his own clinic, as his teachings represented a fundamental change from the values of the tradition.

In addition to the formalized attunement process, Hayashi-sensei is also credited with introducing specific hand positions to treat ailments, an approach that was not generally taught in Usui's original method. Usui, it is said, was disappointed that Hayashi was unable to feel the energy and so developed a simple hand position system in order to give Hayashi the necessary focus. This was not taught to everyone as Usui tailored his teachings to the individual. Hayashi was not interested in the spiritual aspects of Reiki, preferring instead on physical healing alone. This also represented a significant shift in focus for the tradition of Reiki, especially in the Western world as it is one of Hayashi's students that is the undisputed window through which Reiki was transmitted to the West.

Hawayo Takata (born Hawayo Kawamuru) was born to Japanese immigrants on December 24, 1900 on the island of Kauai, Hawaii. She left school after only the second or third grade to work on a sugar cane plantation. She worked hard and eventually married Saichi Takata, the bookkeeper of the plantation.

Hawayo Takata
1900-1980

In 1930 Saichi died leaving her to care for their two children. She had to work very hard with little rest and developed abdominal pains, a lung condition and eventually had a nervous breakdown. Soon after, her sister died.

It was Takata's responsibility to inform her parents of her sister's death and so travelled to Japan to deliver the news. After her task was completed she entered a hospital and learned that she had developed a tumor, gallstones, and emphysema and that she required an operation. She rested for weeks in preparation.

On the day of the operation, while on the table waiting for the doctors, she heard a voice say to her, "This operation is not necessary." She was shocked, as she had never heard voices before, but again it spoke loud and clear, "This operation is not necessary." The third time the voice spoke she arose from the table, wrapped herself in a sheet and asked to speak with her doctor. When her doctor arrived, she asked if there were any alternatives to this operation. The doctor had heard of Hayashi's work and so informed her of his clinic.

At the clinic she began to receive Reiki treatments. She had never heard of Reiki but was slowly beginning to become convinced of its worth, as the diagnosis of the practitioners matched very closely what the doctors had told her.

Each day two practitioners would work with her. The heat from their hands was so strong that she began to wonder if they weren't hiding some sort of apparatus underneath their long, flowing sleeves. One day she grabbed at one of their arms, searching for the device she supposed was there and surprised the practitioner. When she explained what she was doing the practitioner laughed and explained the workings of Reiki to her.

In four months Takata was completely healed. She was so amazed at the results that she decided that she needed to learn this amazing healing technique. However, it was explained to her that Reiki was Japanese, and was intended to stay in Japan. It could not be taught to an outsider.

She spoke to her doctor and asked him to speak to Hayashi on her behalf. Since Hayashi wanted to train another woman in Reiki besides his wife, and in part because Takata was relentless in her pursuit, he decided that she should be trained. In the Spring of 1936 Takata received Reiki I. She worked with Hayashi for one year and was then passed Reiki II. She returned to Hawaii in 1937, followed by Hayashi who then passed Reiki III to her in the Winter of 1938. In 1940, as the cloud of World War II loomed over Japan, Chujiro Hayashi took his own life in the ceremony known as Seppuku rather than participate in violence. Takata was the 13th and last Reiki Master that he initiated.

With the bombing of Pearl Harbor the United States entered the war. Cultural ties to Japan ceased. Reiki existed in the West only through Takata, who then made significant changes to the history, apparently to make it more palatable to a white, largely Christian audience. It is directly from Takata that the false history of Reiki as a Christian healing technique emerged. Altered also were the personal histories of Usui (whom she had never met) and Hayashi; Usui was suddenly a Christian, and had travelled to the United States to attend the University of Chicago. In this historical rewrite, Reiki felt less "foreign" or "scary" to a people at war with the country of its origin. Reiki, she said, had been "lost" to Japan; with the bombings of Hiroshima and Nagasaki the Reiki clinics had been destroyed along with every Reiki Master. Reiki, she said, now only existed with her and it was now her sole responsibility as "Grandmaster" and "Lineage Bearer" (terms not used in Usui or Hayashi Reiki) to keep the tradition alive. But her revisionist history was not the only change that Takata brought to the healing system.

Citing Usui's story of the beggar's quarters, Takata instituted specific fees for sessions and attunements going so far as to say that if these fees were not charged then it "wasn't real Reiki".

The fees for classes/attunements that she charged her students were $250 for Reiki I and $500 for Reiki II. While these fees might not arouse any suspicion of greed, for Reiki III Hawayo Takata charged an incredible $10,000, even going so far as swearing her initiates to an oath to continue the practice lest they violate tradition; to charge less would be to dishonor Reiki. Takata, for a time, was successful in molding Reiki into a franchise system of which she was firmly at the head.

Another change that Takata instituted was to forbid students from taking notes; teaching Reiki strictly as an oral tradition. In her Reiki II classes, when the symbols were taught, she collected the individual practice papers from her students and ritually burned them to ensure that the secret symbols would not be exposed to outsiders.

Regardless of what criticisms we may have of her techniques, it is an undisputed fact that Takata-sensei was successful in preserving and promoting Reiki in the West, and for that she should be honored. She is the originator of the "Usui Shiki Ryoho" which means "the Usui way healing method", the name of the original lineage of Reiki in the West, of which *BlueLotus* is a part.

Before her death in 1980 Takata-sensei initiated 22 Reiki Masters. Their names are reproduced here for posterity:

George Araki	Virginia Samdahl
Barbara McCullough	Dorothy Baba
Beth Grey	Mary McFaden
Ursula Baylow	John Gray
Paul Mitchell	Rick Bockner
Iris Ishitkura	Bethel Phaigh
Fran Brown	Harry Kuboi
Barbara Weber Ray	Patricia Ewing
Ethel Lombardi	Shinobu Saito
Wanja Twan	Kay Yamashita
Phyllis Lei Furumoto	(Takata's Sister)
(Takata's granddaughter)	Barbara Brown

In 1983 several of Takata's students that she had elevated to the Master level gathered in Canada to discuss the future of Reiki. This group became known as "The Reiki Alliance". As part of this meeting, the assembled Reiki Masters shared notes on what they had learned from Takata-sensei and were shocked to learn that while their information was similar, it was indeed different, even down to differences in the symbols they had been passed. It was decided to standardize what they would teach from that point forward even down to the specific fees that would be charged, enshrining the $10,000 Master/Teacher fee as a point of dogma.

Phyllis Furumoto

Another significant development from this meeting was that Takata's granddaughter, Phyllis Furumoto, stepped forward and claimed that she was "Grandmaster and Lineage Bearer" as well as "Sole heir to the Usui system" of Reiki. Whether she initiated this on her own, or was asked to claim it by the newly formed Alliance is unclear.

What *is* clear is that the titles of "Grandmaster" or "Lineage Bearer" were never a part of Usui-sensei's teachings, making Furumoto's claim regarded in some circles as more political posturing then a genuine attempt at preserving tradition.

Barbara Ray

Some Reiki Masters had decided not to attend the Alliance, preferring to keep their practice and teachings autonomous. One of these Masters, Dr. Barbara Ray claimed that *she* was the true successor of Takata, and called her system "Real Reiki"™ (and later "The Radiance Technique"™) claiming that her system was the only authentic, un-fragmented system of Reiki, citing private conversations with Takata in which Ray was allegedly told of (and presumably attuned to) additional levels of Reiki beyond the Master level.

In 1997, in an effort to exert control over how Reiki was taught, Furumoto and the Alliance tried, unsuccessfully, to trademark the term "Reiki", an act that caused further schism between the various lineages.

In the late 1990's, Reiki Masters from the West began to travel to Japan in search of information as to Reiki's origins and practices, and were pleasantly surprised to learn that Reiki had never been lost in its mother country. Usui's clinic had survived and flourished, and the information learned from the Masters there proved to be invaluable. Besides dispelling the myths that Takata had put forward, it was learned that Reiki in Japan is much more intuitive than it is generally practiced in the West, and the specific hand positions normally taught in the Western world are not used, while other meditative practices –attributed to Usui himself –are common place. New information is coming to light all the time as the two cultures slowly begin sharing their insights with the other, ushering in a new golden age of Reiki practice.

MODERN HISTORY, MODERN LINEAGES
Since Reiki has come to the West there has been a veritable explosion of new ideas, thoughts, and practices that have led to new and interesting ways to utilize this divine power. This has led to many, many lineages of Reiki –each with their own name or even "brand" –many purporting to be more powerful or "a higher vibration" than Usui Reiki. This, in my opinion, fails to take into consideration the very personal power that Reiki has. While it is true that many different "flavors" of Reiki might prove to be more powerful for those who are attuned to them, in my experience *it is the practitioner themselves* who actually determines the power that they hold. The practice of Reiki awakens the divine potential within the practitioner, and so these different flavors –while they may indeed be useful –are not necessarily "more powerful" for everyone.

Some of the more popular (or more interesting) schools of Reiki are:

Karuna Reiki
Developed by William Lee Rand this form of Reiki is one that purports to be a "higher" vibration and "more powerful" than Usui Reiki. Has additional symbols for more specific purposes.

Seichim
This is another energy healing system that claims spiritual lineage from ancient Egypt. Channeled by Patrick Zeigler this would appear to be an "extension" of Usui Reiki, using several additional symbols.

Blue Fire Reiki
Founded by Carrie Hammond, this unique school of Reiki has the addition of "blue fire", an energy current utilized by practitioners of the Feri tradition of witchcraft and guided by the Middle Eastern angel/god Melek Ta'us.

Tibetan Reiki
This form of Reiki claims Tibetan linage and has additional symbols.

Rainbow Reiki
Developed by Walter Lübeck and includes the addition of symbols to speak directly to the elements, earth, air, fire, and water as they manifest in the human body and energy field. Also utilizes specific mantras and totem animals in relation to Feng Shui.

Shamballa Reiki
Also called "Shamballa Multidimensional Healing", this technique is used for healing past lives and on all dimensions and combines symbols from other energy systems into its teachings, such as Maha Karuna, Seichim and Terra-Mai.

There are many, many more. An internet search will yield some interesting results. As with all things, use your intuition –and a little research –to guide you.

CHAPTER 3: Philosophy

While in the West much emphasis is placed on physical healing, the Japanese approach is and always has been that of holism; that healing of the body is only part of the total package, along with the mind, emotions, and spirit. To heal, in the Eastern sense, is to bring all of these factors into balance and it is through this natural balance of personal forces that Reiki brings about the desired healing result.

Reiki, unlike other forms of energy work, does not rely on the psychic skills of the practitioner. It is entirely possible to be able to channel Reiki and even pass attunements without possessing the psychic sensitivity necessary to feel the flow of power. Neither does it depend on belief; one can be skeptical about Reiki and still have it work for them, either giving or receiving. This is true because it's *real*; much in the same sense as one doesn't need to believe in electricity in order to have it power their house.

Another point of difference between Reiki and most other psychic healing techniques is that Reiki allows the practitioner to channel divine energy without the need to draw on their own life-force in the process. Since the practices of Reiki allow us to touch into and channel this divine source of power, it is inexhaustible, and will not leave the practitioner drained at the end of a session, unlike some other psychic healing modalities, such as those involved with some forms of Qi Gong.

Reiki is able to assist with physical healing because it treats the very core of the illness by convincing the body to heal itself. The spiritual approach to disease is that it occurs first in the energy-body as *imbalance*, and it is the primary function of Reiki to channel additional life-force into the energy-body so as to restore the body's own natural balance.

The energy that is channeled in a Reiki session is not any different than what can be accessed by any living person. There are, however, fundamental differences between the individual who has been attuned to Reiki and one who has not.

First and foremost the attuned practitioner had undergone a metaphysical experience that has "widened" their energetic channel, granting them a greater capacity for channeling energy in general. It is commonly reported by those who have been attuned that they are suddenly able to channel more energy than they could before (or even that they are now suddenly able to *feel* energy, where perhaps they couldn't prior). The attunement breaks down energetic blocks within us that are preventing us from being able to use energy effectively. While Reiki is certainly not the only path that can grant this experience, it is certainly one of the easiest; one needs only to have the attunement in order to have this inner shift occur.

Yet another major difference is that the attuned practitioner has had their energetic channels "rewired" so that their "default" is to draw from universal (*i.e.* divine) energy, as opposed to their personal life-force. This is an important aspect of working with Reiki as it is this point that prevents the practitioner from becoming depleted at the end of a session, underscoring the precept, "to give Reiki is to receive Reiki"; the practitioner also receives the healing and spiritual benefits of Reiki simply by channeling it in a session.

Reiki will also come when it is needed. Almost all (and maybe even all!) practitioners that I know have reported that their Reiki will just "turn on" at seemingly random times. Often this will manifest as ones hands becoming "hot" or tingling. They can feel it flowing off "somewhere" and sometimes later will have it confirmed that they were in the proximity of someone who was "in need". The conscious decision to channel Reiki is not needed (although it can certainly help). Divine life-force knows where and when it is needed and since this energy has its own consciousness it is perfectly capable of negotiating where and when it will flow.

In Chapter 1 I mentioned that an important tenant of Reiki is that it could do no harm. It is cited so often that it has become a point of dogma; to refute this "fact" will likely invite heavy criticism of your practice, likely in the form of accusations that what you are doing "isn't Reiki". Privately there has been much discussion on whether or not this is actually true, since life-force (even "universal" life-force) is really just a current of power it would stand to reason that this power could be channeled with ill intent, thus causing the very harm that Reiki traditionally claims is impossible.

While some are operating from belief systems that state that only positive intentions carry energetic weight, I can speak from personal experience that this is really just wishful thinking at best, and the result of ignorance and fear at worst.

Energy is energy is energy, and is not subject to any moralistic judgment in order to give it power or momentum. A negative affirmation is just as powerful as a positive one, the "proof" of which should be readily apparent to anyone who has discovered that the root of their recurring problems lays not in back luck or external circumstance, but in the very negative thinking that positive affirmations is attempting to change. We tell ourselves that we are too fat; that we aren't smart enough; we repeat internally any number of self-depreciating statements and attitudes that do nothing but tear down the very foundation of our being. Certainly if negative thoughts were less powerful than positive ones, every meek person could gain the confidence they desired, every individual suffering from poor self-esteem could see their own worth, and every addict could change their ways in an instant.

We often are our own worst enemies: our own thinking can drag us down. But an important lesson in the Age of Aquarius is that thoughts are things; if negative thinking causes negative energy, then positive thinking can do the opposite.

This is a large part of the metaphysical teachings of magical paths, such as ceremonial magic and witchcraft; magic (*i.e.* energy) is simply a tool, what makes it positive or negative is simply ones point of view. A tool has no moral absolute. Is a hammer good or evil? It can help build a house, or it can crush a skull; the judgment is in the DOing, not the BEing.

If Reiki were simply a current of energy, subject to the power of our individual intent then it certainly could do harm, just as it so often heals. But Reiki is not just a current of energy.

Consider again the two words that go into its name; Rei and Ki... meaning *spiritually guided* life-force energy. While life-force can heal or harm equally, the tradition of Reiki by way of the attunement assures that there are spiritual protections in place.

While not part of traditional teachings, my experience is that the energy channeled during a Reiki session is being first channeled by the higher-self of the practitioner and *into the higher self of the recipient*. It is the higher self of the recipient that "makes the decisions" as to how much energy to accept (if any) and where it will ultimately flow. This is very much in line with traditional teachings that state that Reiki will flow where it is needed most and *not* necessarily where the practitioner is intending it.

The higher self of the individual is their deeper, spiritual nature that is most concerned with soul development. It is that part of ourselves that transcends the ego and as such is not concerned with the petty negative attitudes that are at the root of intending another harm. While the practice of Reiki widens our channel for *all* energy, the practices and intention of Reiki is always that of a higher spiritual nature, and as such invokes the presence of the higher self, ensuring protection from ill-intent that would otherwise cause harm.

Consider for a moment the practices of the ancient Kahuna. These ancient Polynesian shamanic practitioners are said to have been able to bless or to curse with equal power. They too recognized that their magical powers were derived from their higher selves (sometimes called the *"aumakua"*) but an interesting point of their practices lies not in their ability to heal, but in how to hex: knowing that their *aumakua* was not interested in harmful magic, the Kahuna had to obtain the energy necessary for their darker workings from another source, and it is said that they found this source of dark power in the enlisting of evil spirits.

While it is certainly possible for any one of us to "turn to the dark side", the spiritual practices associated with Reiki are designed to help us transcend the bonds of the ego; those very bonds that would lead us into the temptation of malevolence. Quite simply, the practices of Reiki keep us aligned to our higher spiritual purpose and thus protect us (and those around us) from the potential ill effects of negative spiritual power. In this we learn that with the power granted to us in the attunement comes the responsibility to use it wisely and for the highest good.

THE REIKI PRINCIPLES
The Five Principles of Reiki are passed down in various forms, depending on one's lineage. These are five concepts that, when taken together, form a sort of spiritual formula that provides the practitioner with a means by which to enter into communion with the divine source and then to channel that force outward, thus mediating divine presence into the world. The Five Principles are derived from a poetic statement written by Usui

which was printed at the beginning of this book. The Principles themselves as given in our lineage are:

> *Just for today, anger not.*
> *Just for today, worry not.*
> *Be grateful.*
> *Work on yourself with appreciation.*
> *Be kind to all living things.*

In order to better understand how this formula works, let us take each part individually:

Just for today, anger not.

The first thing that we should realize when contemplating this principle is that it's *not* saying that we should never be angry. "Just for today" begins this precept, and as such it is telling us that this is more concerned with the present moment than with any sort of ongoing state.

When working in a spiritual path, especially one that is considered "alternative" by the mainstream, it is tempting to fall into the trap of feeling that emotions like anger are "negative", while emotions like love are "positive". In reality emotions carry with them no absolute qualities of "good" or "bad". Emotions are simply energy that runs through and manifests in our psyches; it is what we do with that energy that determines its value. Sometimes anger can be toxic; causing us to remain stuck and becoming a source of pain, suffering, and weakness. At other times anger can be empowering, such as when we see injustices in the world and our anger can inspire us to stand up for what is right. As in all things, it is relative.

In the context of a Reiki session, however, we are being asked to let go of any anger that we may have, just temporarily. Anger is a response to when boundaries have been transgressed, which means that it is a current response to a past act. If yesterday someone wronged me and today I am holding anger, I am allowing my energy to live in the past. I am living in yesterday instead of the now. In this sense, to let go of my anger is to more fully live in the present moment.

Just for today, worry not.

This is the same as the previous principle, except in reverse. Again, we are not being told to "never worry" (a pretty tall order for some of us). We are just being reminded to let it go in the moment. Worry is a form of our energy leaking away by being projecting our awareness into the future. "What might happen to me tomorrow?" Again, we are not living for today. By letting go of our worry and our anger we are in a better position to focus our awareness in the present moment, which is the first step in our spiritual formula. "Be here now."

Be grateful.

We already know the value in "counting our blessings" as part of a spiritual practice. When we are grateful, we enter into a state of expansion in which our energy-body can open up so that our hearts may likewise be open to universal compassion, a necessary step toward being filled with divine presence. Compassion creates an empty space within us –devoid of ego – into which the divine can then flow. Gratitude allows us to transcend the ego, and invite the presence of God Hirself into our lives.

Work on yourself with appreciation.

The Work cited here is with a big 'W', meaning one's purpose; our spiritual work, that which feeds us spiritually. Included in this, of course is little 'w' work, that of our employment; or that which allows us to be fed physically. Whether we choose to specify which type of work we are referring to, this is the recognition that the value is in the doing; we work hard, and we are appreciative for the opportunity. We *Work* hard, and are likewise thankful, even though it might prove difficult.

When working on ourselves we are often confronted with those aspects of our personality that are unpleasant, weak, or fearful. As humans we spend much of our time and energy attempting to *hide* those aspects of ourselves from the light of our consciousness, but the spiritual path requires that we take inventory of what's hidden in the dark; our tools enable us to look beyond our bruised egos or shameful secrets in order to truly *heal*; and only by owning our own totality can we even make the attempt. We are appreciative for the opportunity to work on ourselves, because, in reality, there is no other endeavor as worthy.

Having let go of anger and worry to be mindful in the present moment; having opened our hearts and selves to divinity in gratitude; and having invited the presence of that divinity within us to work on all parts of ourselves, we are now able to fulfill the final part of our formula:

Be kind to all living things.

This is nothing less than allowing ourselves to be the mediators of divine presence. Whether that be in the form of a Reiki session (in which we mediate that divine presence through our hands and into the recipient) or simply by practicing kindness, (random or calculated) we become "priests" or "priestesses" when we make the conscious decision to allow divinity to use us as willing vessels, and assist in making the world a better place in the doing.

Part of making the world a better place, in my opinion, is to learn as much as possible about how it works. We live in a world in which we have access to as much knowledge as we have ever had access to –and with the advent of the internet, in mere seconds! Never before has so much information about the practices of different cultures been so readily available. With the progression of the New Age the spiritual practices of many different cultures and peoples have been given a common area in which to express, mingle, and grow. While traditional practices certainly have a place in rooting us to the past, we can –like the lotus flower –grow beyond the mud of our primal history through the shared waters of existence, striving to bloom in the full light of the sun where all is finally illuminated.

Reiki lets us open up to divine energy in a way to allow it to inform us directly. In this, Reiki becomes a path to enlightenment without the trappings of organized religion. Because of this, Reiki can combine with and inform whatever spiritual, meditative, or healing practices you are already engaged in. Reiki, in this way, becomes a syncretic path; it can allow other modalities, models, and practices to inform itself, making Reiki perfect for everyone, regardless of background or previous experience.

CHAKRAS

One common addition to the practice of Reiki is working with the chakra system. While not a part of Usui's original work, the Hindu chakras are energy centers in the body; the major ones are 7 in number and start at the base of the spine ending at the crown. They detail a progression of spiritual energies as manifested in the physical plane. Psychics and healers work with the chakras as they are associated not only with specific areas of the body, but also certain ailments, physical, emotional, and spiritual.

Each of the chakras are associated with certain colors, stones, musical notes, herbs, and even yogic postures. While a full study of the chakra system would take volumes, below is a brief description of the function of each of these energy centers, and some of their common associations.

Beginning at the base of the spine, the Root chakra is concerned with our primal needs; food, sex, security. Its name in Sanskrit is *Muladhara*, and it is our connection to the physical, and facilitates that state of being known as being 'grounded'. Its color is red and stones associated with it are Garnet, Red Jasper, and Ruby. It's element is Earth.

Beneath the navel, the second or Sacral chakra is named *Swadhisthana* and is concerned with sexuality, specifically the essence of surrender and merging. Its element is Water, and so its energy is best seen in how two droplets of water merge together to make one. Its color is orange and stones include Carnelian, and Orange Calcite.

The third chakra is *Manipura* and is located at the Solar Plexus and deal with issues surrounding our personal power. Confidence, will, courage are all associated with this center. Its color is yellow and stones include Tiger's Eye, Citrine, Amber, and Yellow Jasper.

Anahata, the fourth chakra is the Heart-center and is usually visualized as green. This is our emotional opening to universal compassion. When out of balance it can manifest as being emotionally shut down, or as violent mood-swings. Stones associated with it are Rose Quartz, Green Aventurine, Watermelon Tourmaline, and Jade.

The fifth is the Throat chakra and deals with communication and creative expression. It is seen as blue and stones are Lapis, Sodalite, Angelite, and Turquoise. Its name is *Vishuddha*.

Ajna, the sixth chakra, is called the Third Eye and deals with inner sight, intuition, and psychic power. Traditionally this is visualized as indigo, but many modern practitioners use violet instead. Amethyst and Sugalite are appropriate stones to use for this chakra.

Finally, the Crown chakra is *Sahasrara* and is traditionally violet, but many modern practitioners visualize this as a brilliant white (or white-gold) light. Stones include Clear Quartz, White Topaz, or Herkimer Diamond. This is your connection to the divine source; your own "higher self", and pure consciousness. Issues of spiritual addiction arise when this is out of balance, as well as a feeling of being "cut off" from the spiritual plane.

Reiki practitioners often use their skills to "tune in" to what the body of the recipient is telling them, and a working knowledge of the chakra system can prove quite useful in assisting the practitioner provide a more effective use of session time. By channeling energy into each of the chakras we can assist the recipient to achieve a greater sense of balance, or even address specific mental/emotional/spiritual/physical issues that may be associated with the chakra in question. When the chakras are perceived as being in balance and "spinning" in harmony, then our own energy field will be clear, strong and in balance.

Some practitioners might be inspired to utilize the associated crystals and stones to assist in clearing and charging the chakras. This might be done by placing the stone on the physical body in the area of the associated chakra and then channeling Reiki into the body through the crystal. It is important to use your own intuition and let the Reiki guide you to what is best for the individual situation.

REIKI SPIRIT GUIDES
Another add-on from the New Age is the concept of "Reiki Guides"; beings –perhaps Reiki Masters who have since passed on –that make themselves available from the other side to assist in the work of Reiki. For those lineages that pass this belief system, it is taught that the Reiki Guides serve the tradition of Reiki lending their power as heightened channels for additional Reiki power. This belief likely began sometime in the 1980's when Trance Channeling became vogue. It was also at this time when the Masters that met after Takata's death realized that there were differences in the symbols that had been passed to them. One solution was that the Reiki Guides were believed to be "making corrections" to symbols that were drawn incorrectly, thus ensuring that no matter what variant had been passed one could rest assured that the energy would still be pure.

Before I was attuned to Reiki I had already begun working with energy healing. The form that this practice took at the time involved connecting to spirit guides who acted in the capacity of healers. Using terminology that stemmed from the tradition of Huna, healing practitioners were instructed to connected to these guides and then allow them to place their hands inside our own, thus guiding us to do the work as needed. We worked to restore balance to the auric field by projecting light into the energy body in various colors and vibrations as our intuitions dictated; hot spots were sent a cool blue, while cold spots were warmed up with gold or orange hues. White light was channeled into the aura to finish and we all were amazed at how well our skills increased by working with these guides.

Reiki Guides need not be any different than this. While not part of Usui-Reiki I see no reason to shun thus (or any) practice if it can yield positive results. Likewise if one is not inspired to work in this fashion then there is no reason that one should feel compelled to do so.

CHAPTER 4: PRACTICE

The practices involved in Reiki at the first level are quite simple. Reiki I is really about becoming accustomed to the energy and so the practices at this level tend to be geared toward relaxation, and meditative contemplation.

GASSHO BREATHING

The first exercise (and one that Usui taught to his own students) is called Gassho Breathing. In this exercise the hands are held in the "Gassho position" (i.e. the "prayer position", with hands held together at heart level, palms together, fingers pointed up). Eyes closed, bow in reverence to the divine source in all things and begin to breathe slowly and deeply, paying close attention to your exhale; your outward breath should exit your nose and graze the tips of your fingers. As you continue to breathe, slowly and deeply, allow yourself to remain relaxed and present; should your thoughts drift, just gently bring them back to the tips of your fingers, your breath, and the present moment. Stay in this state for as long as you'd like, preferably a few to several minutes. You may end by again bowing in reverence to the divine, or move on to the next exercise.

CONTEMPLATION OF THE PRINCIPLES

Once we have performed the Gassho Breathing, we can move directly into the Contemplation of the Five Principles of Reiki. After you have adequately relaxed and maintained the Gassho exercise above, begin slowly chanting the Five Principles out loud, taking the time to really feel the impact of each, as you continue to breathe. Notice your thoughts and how you feel. You may wish to chant them multiple times (I prefer to chant them three times, sometimes more) in order to allow deeper parts of your consciousness to open up to the experience. When completed, bow in reverence to the divine source.

Traditionally this exercise should be performed in the morning first thing after waking, and at night just before retiring.

WATERFALL MEDITATION

This exercise was first taught to me by my husband, Chas Bogan, also a Reiki Master. Just before he was about to perform a Reiki session with a client, he spontaneously experienced the visual and sensation of a brilliant waterfall of light, flowing from the heavens above. This power, which he felt was a symbolic representation for divine life-force (aka Reiki) entered into his crown chakra and then flowed down into his heart, splitting into two rivers of light and love that moved left and right into each arm and then flowed out through his hands. He felt that after experiencing this visual form for a few moments that his Reiki was flowing bright and clear.

I found this visual exercise to be extremely helpful in preparing for a Reiki session in that it helped to get energy flowing, as well as being an exercise of personal purification.

As an interesting aside, I later learned that there is a sacred waterfall on Mt. Kurama, the birthplace of Reiki where Usui had his mystical experience. The Zen monks there reportedly would stand underneath this waterfall and allow it to flow over their crown to cleanse and open then up to the divine. Chas was not aware of this when he had the experience.

To perform this exercise I would recommend that you first perform Gassho Breathing, and then chant the Principles, moving then into the visualization as described above. When you feel that your Reiki is flowing strongly you may open up your arms so that your palms are facing upward, basking in the glow of light and love that Reiki brings. You may now begin your session or whatever other work you had planned.

CONDUCTING A SESSION

While there is no one right way to perform a Reiki session, there are certainly some guidelines that can be observed to help make the experience as powerful and positive as possible. Likely you will find your own style of practice along the way.

SETTING UP THE SPACE

The physical space in which you work is important. Doing a session in a clean, quiet space will be much different than if performed in a cluttered room with a lot of activity going on. The space should ideally be one in which both the practitioner and recipient can effectively relax and enjoy what is about to transpire. This can mean making sure that the space is clean; both physically and well as spiritually. Too often I have found spiritual practitioners relying on burning sage and other methods of purifying the energy of a space when what is *really* needed is a good old fashioned washing. Dust, vacuum, wipe down the baseboards... make sure that the space is *clean*. Working in an environment that is dirty is not conducive to performing any spiritual session, especially not one that is geared toward achieving a sense of purity and balance. A dirty or cluttered space is at the best distracting, and at the worst just plain gross. Neither state bodes well for the receptiveness of the work. Do yourself and your client a favor and clean your room before you invite them in.

In addition to clutter being a distracting influence so can a lot of noise or unrelated activity. While Reiki can of course be performed anywhere (and indeed the needs of the moment should outweigh any environmental restrictions that you may find yourself subject to) it is preferable to maintain a sense of quiet and calm in your working space. Some practitioners utilize relaxing music (some appropriate titles appear in the resources section at the end of this book) or what is commonly called a "white noise machine". This can help to create an environment of controlled sound so that outsides noises will be less distracting or even completely unnoticed. Music creates a sense of peace and calm and can help both practitioner and client to better enter into that state that is conducive of a good and relaxing Reiki session.

One other thing to consider is engaging the sense of smell. If your space is clean then it should be free of any odors that would prove unpleasant and therefore a barrier to the work. Many practitioners will use aromatherapy to provide both a pleasant scent as well as to alter the energy of the space, depending on what scents are used. Be aware, however, that some people are quite sensitive to scents and for these individuals it would be advisable to not add any scents to the room. If in doubt ask your client!

While some practitioners might work with the sense of smell by utilizing incense, one thing to consider is that *incense has smoke particulates which are actually toxic*. Recent scientific research has determined that *all* smoke is carcinogenic to some degree, and while it is still possible to work with incense in a way that is relatively safe (providing that it is burned in a well ventilated room and in amounts that do not outweigh the capacity of that ventilation) any smoke in your lungs is too much from a health stand-point. For this reason alone I personally advise against using it in a Reiki session. Essential oils, in my opinion, are the way to go.

True essential oils are the highest vibration of the plant and as such are perfect for working with the spiritual energies of the plants (sometimes called "the plant spirit"). One easy way to work with essential oils is to use a *diffuser*. A simple version if this consists of a base with a (usually) removable dish or bowl on top, underneath which is placed a tea-lite candle. Fill the dish almost all the way with water and then add a few to several drops of your favorite essential oils. Light the candle and as the water is warmed and begins to evaporate the oils will be gently diffused into the room, creating a nice (and clean!) scent and imbibing the room with their particular vibration.

Different herbs and plants carry different energies and affect our energy fields in different ways. While the art of aromatherapy is beyond the scope of this volume, familiarizing yourself with some basic scents can help to provide a space that is better suited to healing and to spiritual development.

What follows is a (very) short list of some of my favorite essential oils and what they can be used for in a Reiki session.

Lavender
Used to bring balance and calm to a room. Sometimes used to help induce sleep, if used when feeling down or sluggish lavender can actually "perk you up"; not in an anxious way, but in a supportive and balanced way. This is probably the number one scent that is sold at my shop and is used for a variety of purposes.

Sandalwood
This is an excellent scent for *grounding*; for pulling one's energy back into the body and creating a sense of calm focus. Excellent for mediation and healing work. My Reiki Master suggested adding a drop to each palm and rubbing briskly before performing a Reiki session.

Jasmine
This creates a sense of peace and of open-heartedness and is excellent for spiritual work, especially that of recognizing unity with all life. It raises one's spiritual vibrations and can be used in order to access one's "higher self" which is helpful when working with Reiki which depends on the higher self connection in order to determine how and where the energy will flow.

Lemon
Used for spiritual cleansing, lemon is also a natural anti-depressant; it supports our mental state, create a calm opening

that is both gentle and stable. Excellent for use in sessions in which grief or fear is an issue.

Rue

This powerful herb is used to dispel negativity and so can be used to cleanse a space or a person, especially when that space of person has suffered any level of trauma or negative event.

Combinations of essential oils can be blended in order to utilize many different spiritual vibrations. Experiment to see what scents you like best.

Once the physical needs of the space of been addressed then it is important to make sure that the spiritual needs are likewise met. Having been cleaned and made free of distraction, and having then been set with the desired energy using scent (if desired) it is important to energetically cleanse and charge the space with Reiki. This can easily be done simply by opening up to Reiki and allowing the energy to flow through your hands and into the four walls, the ceiling, the floor, and finally the center of the space. As you start with one of the walls, project Reiki into that area (not just the physical wall, but the entire area in front of it, as well) and then when you feel it is "complete" move along to the next wall and do the same until all four walls have been charged. Send Reiki above and then to below and then finally to the center, which then is seen to expand and fill up the entire room or working area with Reiki light, making it more conducive for the work that is about to happen. A Reiki charged room feels great, and will be free of energetic forms that might be distracting to the work performed.

MINDFULNESS PREPARATION

Once the space has been set up, and the recipient has settled in and led to relax, take a moment to allow yourself to come back into the present moment by performing the Gassho Breathing.

Before a session I also recite the Five Principles, and then engage in the Waterfall Mediation. Then you're ready to go!

THE SESSION ITSELF

Once the recipient is on the table or sitting comfortably in a char and you are ready to begin there are a couple of different approaches that you might employ. Neither is more correct than the other and likely you will at times utilize both methods at some point. Both have their own pros and cons and so being aware of these potentials and limitations is a necessary part of one's Reiki training.

Aura Method

This method is my preferred method. When working in the aura you are actually keeping your hands *above* the physical body, sending Reiki into the energy-field of the recipient which then affects the physical body as well. My preference for this method is largely because when I work in this way I am more able to sense the energy of the person's body and aura and so am better able to follow my intuition as to where to place my hands. I often will feel little sensations in certain places that tell me that "something is going on" there. This can range from spots of heat or cold, and even to slight electric tingling and even full-on visual and psychic impressions that suddenly flood my consciousness.

Feather-Touch Method

The Feather-Touch method quite literally is allowing your hands to rest on the physical body of the recipient "as light as a feather", that is to say without applying pressure of any kind. Some practitioners find that they prefer to lightly touch the areas of the body when sending Reiki as it connects them in a deeper way to the client and helps to "ground" the energy in the body. This can be extremely helpful in cases in which a person is suffering from tension headaches and needs to have their energy redistributed, in which case lightly touching the feet often helps. When utilizing this method it should go without saying that there are certain areas of the body that should never be touched, such as breasts in women, and the buttocks and genitals. Another problem area is the front of the throat which can actually prove to be stressful for the recipient. For these areas the Aura Method is always preferred.

Regardless of which method you prefer to use there are a couple of guidelines to consider in terms of posture and the specific way in which to hold the hands. I was taught that when giving Reiki one should hold their hands much in the same way as one would while swimming; slightly cupped, with fingers held together. This is to help to focus the energy channel (minor chakra) in the palms of the hands to better facilitate the flow of the Reiki. Reiki will flow equally through either hand although you may intuitively decide to sometimes use just one hand on the person while the other might be held upward much like an "antennae" to better channel the divine flow. Experiment, and see what works best for you.

Your posture should be to stand with the spine straight, knees slightly bent with the feet about shoulder's width apart, and the tailbone tucked forward so as to more fully open the energy channels of the body. This might seem awkward at first, but with practice this will prove to be second nature as your body adjusts to the new positions.

Byosen Reikan-ho (Scanning)
The method for sensing imbalances with the hands
This is a technique that looks for "the source of the fire", aka the origin of illness in the body. "Byosen" can be translated as "line of sickness" and is the vibration of energy that is emitted from an area that is tense, blocked, or dis-eased. This is perceived by the Reiki practitioner in various levels and, according to Frank

Arjava Petter, are five in number[2]. These levels of *byosen* indicate the seriousness of the condition. They are (from the lowest to the most serious):

1. **Heat.** This is perceived as being above normal body temperature.
2. **Extreme heat.** This is of the type that causes your palms to sweat.
3. **Tingling.** This can have an almost electric feeling, or feel that your hands are becoming numb or falling asleep. This level can also be felt as a magnetic pull or resistance.
4. **Pulsation or cold.** The pulsation can be strong or weak, slow or fast. This can also manifest as "cold spots".
5. **Pain,** usually in the hand or arm of the practitioner, but occasionally elsewhere. This is the most serious level of *byosen* and usually manifests in the hand, all the way up to the shoulder, but might appear anywhere in the body, corresponding with areas of the body of the client.

Usui taught this technique to his students as a practice designed to allow the practitioner to learn how to better perceive the energy of the client, giving the practitioner information about the state of the client beyond what is gleaned by normal methods of communication. Sometimes misconstrued as being intuitive or psychic, *byosen* scanning is a skill that can be learned simply by increasing one's awareness and involves taking in all of the information available to our physical senses. What follows is my version of this simple and effective technique.

- Begin by connecting to Reiki. Imagine the light of divine love and healing pouring through you and shining outward.

---

[2] *Reiki News* Magazine, Vol. 6 #2, Summer 2007.

- For the mental intention to begin the process of scanning the client. You might think to yourself, "I begin Byosen Reikan-ho now." Rub your hands together briskly to get the energy flowing.
- Place your hands over the client's crown, about 2" above the body. Allow your awareness to be soft and open; do not *try* to perceive *anything*; just allow whatever sensation to flow as they will.
- Slowly pass your hands downward over the client's body. Notice any instances of *hibiki*; the Japanese term for "energy vibration". This is the dissonance that occurs when the positive energy of the Reiki practitioner intersects with the negative energy of the dis-ease. Allow your hands to remain in these areas, giving Reiki until the *hibiki* is dissolved and disappears, usually after a repeating and diminishing pattern.
- Repeat this process until the entire body has been scanned.
- Finish by intending, "I have completed Byosen Reikan-ho." Or simply, "Scanning off", or similar.

THE HAND POSITIONS

What has become the standard hand positions in the West was actually not a part of the original Usui teachings. They were first introduced by Usui specifically for Hayashi, who Usui realized was not able to feel the energy and so had trouble following his intuition, which up until that point was how Reiki was taught. Since Hayashi was taught in this manner, this is how he taught his students and so this of course is how Hawayo Takata learned and passed on Reiki to the West.

I will go on record stating that I do not use the formal Western hand positions in my practice as I personally find them to be a barrier to following my intuition (*i.e.* "being in the present moment") and a barrier to performing Reiki in general. I prefer to follow the path of *Reiji*, that of "guidance of spirit" in my work. I realize, however, that while there may be many other people like myself, there are also those, like Hayashi, who may not be able to follow their intuition effectively, or who simply learn differently, and so I pass on the formal Western hand positions to my students but do not require that they be learned or used. They can be helpful should you find yourself in a situation in which you feel "stuck" while giving a session. For this reason, and the sake of completeness, I reproduce the formal hand positions here, along with some common ailments that they are taught to be effective for.

There are twelve basic hand positions as taught in many versions of Western Reiki for use in a session. (Some lineages have more, others less.) For convenience, the body is divided into three sections: the Head, the Front of the Body and the Back of the Body. Each section has four positions giving us the total 12 positions. In traditional Western Reiki these positions are performed in order to maximize the energy flow.

Each position listed here is labeled with a letter: H for positions on Head, F for positions on the Front of the Body, and B for positions on the Back of the Body. They are also each numbered from 1 to 4.

In the Head section (H), the energy is sent into the brain and eyes, nose and the thyroid gland giving the recipient a sense of peace and relaxation.

In the Front of the Body section (F), the energy is sent to the thymus (the central organ of the immune system) to the bladder and the genitals and through the abdominal organs to adjust the body's overall balance.

In Back of the Body section (B), the energy is sent into the shoulders and along the spine to the kidneys and adrenal gland.

Start. To the traditional system I have added this position which I use to start a session. One hand in front of 3rd eye and the other on the crown. This balances the client's energy and calms them, making them more receptive to the energy.

H-1 (Front of the face, over the eyes): Pain in the eyes, nose, mouth, and chin. Balance and concentration. Stress. Raises spiritual vibration.

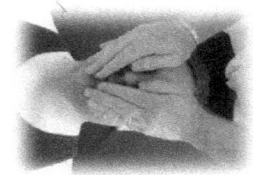

H-2 (Sides of the head): Pituitary and pineal glands. Adjust hormones in the brain. Headaches. Balances the left and right brains. Stress. Improves memory. Expands consciousness. Improves intuition.

H-3 (Back of the head) Base of the brain, spine, and cerebellum. Improving language and eyesight. Adjusting weight. Relaxation. Creativity. Releasing fear.

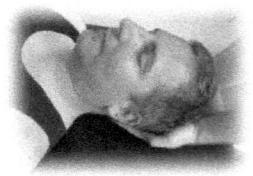

H-4 (Throat): Circulation, lymph, thyroid gland. Blood pressure, metabolism. Confidence, peace, stability, joy, happiness. Improving creativity & communication.

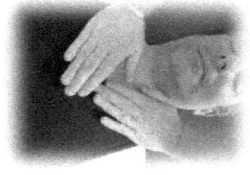

F-1 (Thymus): Circulation, the heart, lungs and thymus. Confidence and mental balance, release stress, improving receptivity. Love, bliss, stability and harmony.

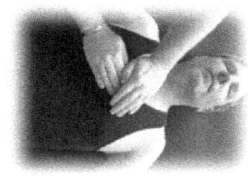

F-2 (Upper belly): Liver, stomach, gallbladder, spleen, digestive system. Anxiety, fear, stress. Relaxation, peace, balance, higher dimensional energy.

F-3 (Below belly button): Liver, pancreas, gallbladder, spleen, colon. Reduce stress, anxiety. Confidence. Receptivity.

F-4 (Genitals): Colon, small intestine, bladder, ovaries, womb, sex organs, prostate gland, excretion. Release anxiety, fear and tension. Expand consciousness.

B-1 (Shoulder blades): Same as F-1. Neck disorders, spinal column, nervous system.

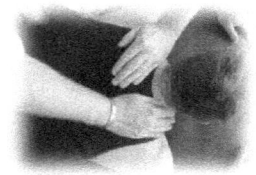

B-2 (The upper back): Same as F-2. Thoracic vertebrae, spinal column and nervous system. Release tension.

B-3 (The lumbar vertebra): Same as F-3. Kidneys, adrenal gland, lumbar vertebra, spinal column, nervous system.

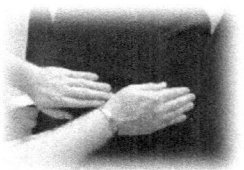

B-4 (Base of spine): Same as F-4. Bones of the lower body such as the bottom of the spine, the coccyx and the pubis and the nervous system. Grounding. Stability.

COMPENSATION

This has been a point of dissent amongst Reiki practitioners probably almost as long as Reiki has been practiced. Citing the story of the Beggar's Quarters, Hawayo Takata insisted that clients pay for Reiki sessions and attunements or else it "wasn't Reiki", saying that those who did not pay for the work would not value it. While there is certainly something to be said about the psychology involved, to state that it "isn't Reiki" if performed for free is both ignorant and offensive; many people who are in need of healing are not able to provide monetary payment and so if payment is required in all cases then what we end up doing is enshrining a system in which healing is only available for the wealthy. *BlueLotus* makes no judgment on whether or not its practitioners charge for their services, preferring to stress the importance of being in the present moment, which would grant an opportunity to make up our minds for ourselves in each situation.

I charge for Reiki sessions. At present (2010) I charge $45 for a half hour session, and $75 for a full hour. Distant sessions are also $45. In addition to these paid, private sessions, I also host a "Reiki Share" which is a public group that meets to share Reiki with each other. For this monthly event we ask for a small donation to help cover costs, but no one is turned away for lack of funds. In this I feel that I am able to "give back" to the community, but am also able to maintain a practice that provides me with necessary financial compensation so that I can continue to eat and pay my bills. In this I find a balance, which I find the essence of Reiki to be all about.

HEALING CRISES

During or after a Reiki session (and especially after an attunement) there is the possibility of enduring what has been dubbed a "Healing Crises". This is an event in which toxins – physical, mental, emotional, and spiritual –begin to arise where once they were previously buried. This is really the body and spirit dealing with those issues that have been buried and so is a type of cleansing or purging of these negative energies. In this case it is possible for the recipient to experience stress that may manifest as aches, pains and even flu-like symptoms. Alternatively this may manifest as the resurfacing of repressed memories, or emotions that are difficult to deal with. Occasionally a client may start crying while on the table or begin feeling ill. It is important that if this happens that you encourage the client to talk about what they are feeling. Lovingly listen to their problems and offer any inspirations that may come to you but not in the form of a diagnosis or advice. If you perceive a medical condition then suggest that they see a doctor to address the situation.

If the issue is psychological then allow the client to talk and depending on the severity of the situation you might suggest that they seek help from a qualified psychologist. In any event after such an episode make sure that the client drinks plenty of water afterward and you might even give them a bit of chocolate or something sweet to help them ground.

During the period immediately following a session (usually three days to a week) or an attunement (sometimes as long as 21 days) it is important to take extra care with yourself, including continuing to drink lots of water in order to help flush these toxins out of your system before they can "get stuck", causing the aforementioned crises to occur.

ENDING A SESSION
When a session is concluded it is a good idea to "disconnect" from the energy of the recipient to make sure that you are not "taking on" any of the energy of that person. To achieve this I perform the following two steps:

Auric Clearing
This is a simple process in which I draw the energy of the recipient's higher self into and through their body to act as a sort of energetic blessing. This also serves to cleanse and "fluff" the aura, providing a sense of balance and well being, while at the same time slightly invigorating the client to bring them gently back from the deep relaxed state that they have likely been experiencing during the session, since they will likely soon need to get up and be on their way.

Letting the recipient know that we are about to complete the session, I instruct them to take three deep breaths while visualizing a brilliant white (or deep blue) light of their higher self hovering above their head. As I inhale in unison with the client, I reach physically and energetically into the area above their head, then "drag" this energy down and through their body as I *quickly* exhale, feeling the energy of their higher self flood into and through their body, cleansing, energizing, balancing, and grounding them in their deeper purpose. I do this three times before moving on to the final step.

Dry Bathing

This is simply a ritual act that is intended to disconnect the energy of the practitioner from that of the recipient. It can be as simple as shaking your hands as if you are shaking droplets of water off of them, or by using the following formula that was passed to me by my Reiki Master:

Begin by placing your right hand on your left shoulder and dragging it diagonally downward to the right over your heart-center. Repeat the process with your left hand on your right shoulder and doing the same action in reverse. This is to make certain that your heart-center (which is the chakra most concerned with intimacy and emotional connection) has been effectively "cleansed" or disconnected from the client. Finish the process by rubbing your hands together as if you are washing them. Bow in reverence to the divine nature (the Buddha nature) of the client. It is done.

You will likely find your own style of working as you practice giving Reiki to others. More important than the actual form is the intention followed by some ritual act. You might achieve that same effect by reciting a poem, or performing some other action that is meaningful to you. As long as you are able to energetically disconnect from the recipient then that is all that matters.

ADDITIONAL USES

Reiki can be used in many ways for a variety of purposes besides simply hands-on healing. Reiki can be given to anyone or anything and will increase its spiritual vibration. When Reiki is given to "inanimate"[3] objects (crystals, stones, jewelry, food or anything else) the charge will usually last about 24-48 hours depending on the substance. (Natural objects tend to hold a charge longer; manufactured objects, such as plastic, tend to hold the charge for only a short time.)

While you will likely find your own style of practice when it comes to working with Reiki is this way, what follows are a few simple guidelines based on my own experiences.

Charging Crystals
At Level One, Reiki can be used to charge crystals and stones prior to use (be sure to cleanse them first by placing in salt or salt water, depending on the type of stone). Holding a cleansed stone in your hand (or holding both hands over the stone) send Reiki into the stone until you intuitively feel the stone "waking up"; I usually perceive this as a soft light that gently lights up within the stone. When this occurs the stone has been charged and may be more effectively used for spiritual work. Additionally, you may wish to send a particular intent into the stone along with Reiki. This becomes more effective at Level Two, but may certainly be done with Reiki I.

REIKI FOR SPIRITUAL DEVELOPMENT

As stated before, Reiki is much more than just a method for what we understand as "healing" in the West. Reiki is a secular

---

[3] I place this in quotes as a reminder that all things that exist carry a type of life-force. All matter is comprised of energy and all energy has consciousness.

system for enlightenment, and as such it is encouraged to work with Reiki specifically for this purpose. Again, this is increased at Level II (and especially at Level III, the Master Level) but Level I practitioners will find that their spiritual practice and development will be greatly increased after working with Reiki. There are many different exercises for working Reiki for spiritual development, both traditional and modern. Some examples of both are given below:

Nentatsu-ho

This is a traditional Japanese method for using Reiki to transform bad habits or thoughts by empowering positive thoughts or affirmations.

- Begin by performing the Gassho exercise.
- Identify some negative thought or habit that you would like to change. Decide what its "opposite" would be and focus on this positive affirmation.
- Place your dominant hand on the occipital ridge (where the skull meets the spine). Allow Reiki to flow freely.
- When your intuition inspires you to continue to the next step, leaving your dominant hand where it is, place your non-dominant hand on the forehead, at the hairline.
- Let the Reiki flow and repeat your positive affirmation. Stating it out loud is best, and in the present tense. ("I am successful and prosperous", NOT "I want prosperity.") Do this several times in a state of non-judgment and gratitude.
- When you feel that you are done, perform the Gassho once more

Working with Reiki Guides

This simple exercise can assist you in connecting with a Reiki Guide, should you wish to work in this way. If not, simply skip this exercise and move on.

- Begin with Gassho Breathing. Recite the Principles and visualize the Waterfall of Light.
- Open your arms, palms facing up. As Reiki projects into your body, allow it to radiate upward from your palms, and also up into and through your third eye and crown chakras.
- State your intent clearly. (*i.e.* "I call to the Reiki Guides to assist me in deepening the Great Work.")
- Sit quietly and notice any subtle shifts or changes in your body or emotions. Take your time with this.
- Continue to allow Reiki to flow through you. You may notice that you get a visual image in your mind's eye of a being. Should this happen do not become surprised or alarmed. Simply sit quietly and begin a dialogue, if you wish. Ask them their name, and ask them if they have come to you to assist you with Reiki.
- If you receive a name then spend some time exchanging Reiki with them before closing.
- If you do not receive a name, politely ask them to go and return when they are willing or able to come to you in a clear and clean way.
- Close by returning to the Gassho position, and bowing in reverence.

Working with Death & Dying

In addition to using Reiki to improve one's overall health, it is also a practice that can be used to help ease the transition from life into death.

We live in a death-phobic culture. All too often we find that our attitudes, and the attitudes of the medical profession, exist around the central idea that life must be preserved and extended at all costs. While on the surface this seems to be reasonable we must also accept that death is the natural conclusion of all life;

death –when it comes for us –is not the enemy. Resistance against the inevitable is. When I am old, should my organs begin the process of failing, I want to be able to transition with dignity, not be hooked-up to a machine that will keep my body alive while my consciousness remains trapped in a decaying prison.

Reiki, being first and foremost a spiritual practice, recognizes that it is the *quality* of life that really matters, and that the physical end of life is not the end of the spirit.

Reiki can bring peace to an otherwise frightening situation. The gentle energy of light and love can help to relive the fears of the dying person and make them better prepared to meet the Great Mystery with dignity, instead of sadness and fear. This is especially true for Reiki Levels Two and Three, but even at Reiki I we can provide gentle love and support to those who need it most: the dying person, and their loved ones.

As for an actual practice, I feel that this especially should be largely intuitive. You may need to Reiki the room itself, but if you cannot then just send loving energy to the dying person and see them bathed in beautiful, soft white light. If they are conscious then they may wish to talk; to tie up whatever loose ends they may perceive. Keep them calm. Talk to them; sing to them; reassure them. Hold their hand if you can. Physical touch, if possible, can be an important aspect of this work. And bathe them in loving Reiki all the while to being them peace and the stability that they need to meet their Maker with an open, and light, heart.

CHAPTER 5: ETHICS AND LEGALITY

One question that often comes up in discussion with Reiki practitioners is whether or not it is ethical to give Reiki before asking permission. In my training in various spiritual traditions I have often heard that it is necessary to ask someone's permission before sending them healing, blessings, etc. To do otherwise, some say, is interfering with the free-will of the recipient. In this mode of thinking, it would be necessary to ask permission before sending Reiki to an individual lest you interfere with their free-will.

It is not the place of *BlueLotus*, or anyone for that matter, to dictate to anyone what they should or should not do in any particular situation. As sentient beings it is up to us to decide for ourselves what we should do. With this in mind I give you the following to consider: To decide that it is *always* necessary to ask for permission before giving Reiki is a type of blanket rule which, when evenly applied to every situation, *brings us out of the present moment;* we are then relying on a static decree that effectively traps our awareness in the past. If the practices of Reiki are geared toward being in the present moment, then it seems to me that in the present moment is where we will find our answers to whatever questions may arise in a given situation. The decision of whether or not to give Reiki, then, is situational.

This becomes more important at Reiki II where distant healing is taught, but the ethics involved are just as relevant at Level I.

Another point that is important to consider is what terms we use to describe ourselves. I have known of some Reiki practitioners who use the term "Reiki Therapist", which I believe gives a false impression. Unless you are a licensed therapist then it is not advisable to use the term lest someone become confused as to what services you are providing.

The same goes for the term "healer". Besides being blatantly false (the Reiki practitioner is not doing the healing; the recipient's own body in conjunction with the Reiki energy, directed by their higher self, is) it has the potential of giving "false hope" to those in need. Reiki has been known to be a catalyst for intense and seemingly miraculous healing, but sometimes a disease cannot be healed with Reiki. When someone is very ill it is possible that they might become desperate, and using a term like "healer" might override any common sense that they may have had previously, leaving both them, and you, open to some difficulty should the Reiki sessions not prove effective. Better to use the term "Reiki practitioner" which covers what we are actually doing; practicing Reiki. All effects of said Reiki are then to be determined by the actual sessions, not by any preconceived terminology.

One last point of legal concern applies to those who prefer to use the feather-touch method in their sessions. When applying Reiki to any part of the body (in our hypothetical situation we will call this "Position 1") and then we wish to change positions (to "Position 2") then it is important that we *lift the hands from the body, move them from Position 1 to Position 2 and then lower the hands back to feather-touch contact with the physical body*. This seemingly simple piece of advice is so important that I am going to say it again. *Lift the hands from the body, move them from Position 1 to Position 2 and then lower the hands back to feather-touch contact with the physical body*. The reason that this is important is that if we simply move our hands from Position 1 to Position 2 while touching the body (even lightly, as in the feather-touch method) it can be *legally construed as massage* and there is the potential for legal action should you perform massage without a license. Do yourself (and your clients) a favor and make sure to follow this simple rule.

CHAPTER 6: THE ATTUNEMENT

The Reiki Level One attunement (like any type of energetic initiation) will manifest in different ways for everyone. In the beginning of this book I described my own experience with this ceremony. While this is not an uncommon experience your own may be quite different. Even so, there are certain things to expect during, and after, the event itself.

During the Attunement
The person to be attuned is seated in a chair and assumes the Gassho position with both feet flat on the floor. There is no talking during the ceremony which can take anywhere from 5 to 15 minutes, depending on various factors. When receiving the attunement you simply have to relax, and perform the Gassho breathing. Should your thoughts wander, simply and gently bring them back to the present moment, as in the Gassho exercise.

At this point I generally recite the Five Principles and perform some energetic adjustments to the space in which we are in so as to create a better energetic environment for the attunement to take place. When I am ready to begin actually passing the attunement I stand behind the recipient and begin the process.

At this point you may feel Reiki on your shoulders, neck, and head area before I lightly place my hands on top of your head. I will use the power of breath through your crown chakra and then tap your left shoulder twice to signal you to raise your hands above your head –still in the Gassho (prayer) position. Don't worry, I will guide them into place.

After I have completed the work in the back I then move to the front, kneeling before the recipient and guiding the hands back into place, then opening them like a book. This is where I attune your hands and you will feel me tapping your palms three times on each. I then guide the hands back once more and then attune your third eye, again tapping three times. I seal up with a breath of power and then return to the back where I complete the work on the head. At this time I will announce when it is complete and you will then be a Reiki Level One Practitioner.

After the Attunement
Immediately after the attunement you may feel spacey, blissful, tingly, warm, or have any number of sensations. The experience is entirely unique to you and so it is up to you to pay attention to any differences that you may feel from your normal waking state. If you are feeling particularly spacey or ungrounded then you may wish to move or stretch or even have something to eat in order to "bring you back into your body", especially if you are to be driving shortly afterward. One thing that is *always* important to do after an attunement, however, is to drink plenty of water.

Sometimes, after the initial sensations of the attunement fade, the initiate can be tempted to become lazy when it comes to their spiritual practices and self-care. It is extremely important that you maintain your practices for (at least) the next 21 days. (I was told 30 days by my Master, but 21 tends to be what has become "traditional"; 21 mimicking the time that Usui spent fasting on Mt. Kurama.) This time period is when the attunement "gels" or sets into place. If you perform your exercises now, then your Reiki will grow in leaps and bounds.

During this time period make sure to perform the following:

- Gassho Breathing
- Waterfall Meditation
- Reciting (and meditating on) the Five Principles
- Practice giving Reiki to yourself by placing your hands on your body, either intuitively or by following the standardized hand positions.

- Practice giving Reiki to others. If you are not able to give Reiki to others, then practice giving Reiki to your food and drink before eating, to your houseplants or trees in your yard, or even pieces of jewelry or crystals. You can give Reiki to anything. The important thing right now is to simply practice letting it flow through your hands as much as possible.

One simple (as well as easy and just plain nice) way to use Reiki is to simply allow it to flow through your hands as you are going to sleep at night; placing your hands on your body and letting the Reiki flow until you drift off. This can improve the quality of your sleep and you may find that your dreams are more vivid.

CHAPTER 7: LINEAGE

When someone is attuned to Reiki they are adopted into a type of "spiritual family" that is recorded with a lineage. All practitioners of Reiki can trace their lineage back to Mikao Usui, and those who were trained in the West can trace to him through Hawayo Takata. (The only exception to this are some who trace their lineage through Diane Stein who claims that she did not receive a certificate for her Reiki Master/teacher attunement and so her lineage begins with her.)

A shorter lineage is no better than a longer one. It is no way indicates how powerful a practitioner you will be; only practice and dedication can determine that. One's lineage is something to be proud of. Far from being a mark of hierarchy it is an acknowledgment of respect for our teachers, and for our teacher's teachers. We honor those who have brought these teachings to us and in so doing we also acknowledge their individual contributions that they have brought; many practitioners have added their own insights and practices into what they teach (myself included) and so each of their "downline" receives the benefit of their unique perspectives and so are honored in the lineage.

My lineage is printed on the following page. If you are (or are to be) attuned by me then this is your lineage too. Notice that ours is a "dual"; with Jeffery A. Martin being attuned by two different Masters. This, as I was told, was because he wanted to have energetic access to the Tibetan symbols and energy in addition to his previous Usui-style Reiki attunement. He was re-attuned and thus was empowered to pass on this additional material, making our lineage Usui/Tibetan in style.

BlueLotus Reiki Lineage

Dr. Mikao Usui

Dr. Chujiro Hayashi

Mrs. Hawayo Takata

Phyllis Lei Furumoto
|
Carol Farmer
|
Leah Smith
|
William Lee Rand

Dr. Barbara Ray
|
Maureen O'Sullivan
|
Kate Hushson Law
|
Vicki Davis
|
Jeannie Greening

Jeffery A. Martin

Anthony Agee

Gary Mills

Lucy Vincze

Kevin Moscrip

Edward Gutierrez

Storm Faerywolf

CHAPTER 8: CONCLUSION & RESOURCES

By now you will have learned that Reiki can be a powerful catalyst for your own growth and healing and can be used by anyone, anywhere, at anytime. If you work diligently with the exercises in this book then you will find that your strength in the power will grow and take you to new places of spiritual development. As a Reiki Level One practitioner you should also feel encouraged to experiment with your new abilities in as many ways as possible. Research Reiki from many different sources. Read books, magazines, attend Reiki shares, talk to people in your local communities about how they do Reiki and what practices they find helpful. You will likely learn many new and interesting methods for applying Reiki to your spiritual practices, and your daily life.

Remember that you will get as much out of Reiki as you put in, which really is a good rule for life. It is my fervent hope that you find this path to be as helpful –and as healing –as I have.

Waterfall above
Rejoicing in the moment
One with light of God.

Books
- *The Spirit of Reiki* by Walter Lübeck, Frank Arjava Petter, and William Lee Rand
- *Magic of Reiki* by Christopher Penczak
- *Hands of Light* by Barbara Brennan

Music
- *Reiki Gold: The Ultimate Reiki Album, Vol. 2*
- *Reiki River* by Niall
- *Celestial Reiki* by Jonathan Goldman & Laraaji

Other projects by Storm Faerywolf:

The Mystic Dream is my online store. Visit www.TheMysticDream.com for more information and to peruse our books, crystals, and handmade spiritual and magical products.

Our online school offers long-distant and downloadable classes in various spiritual and magical modalities including Black Rose Witchcraft, Modern Conjure, Spiritual Cleansing, BlueLotus Reiki, and more! Visit www.TheMysticDreamAcademy.com for more info.

I am also a regular contributor to Modern Witch, a website, blog, and podcast. Check out www.ModernWitch.com.

Signed copies of my books can be purchased from www.TheMysticDream.com:

The Stars Within the Earth
Poetry, spells, and art inspired by the F(a)eri(e) tradition of witchcraft.

Betwixt & Between: Exploring the Faery Tradition of Witchcraft

Forbidden Mysteries of Faery Witchcraft

Awakening the BlueLotus: A Reiki Level One Handbook

Becoming the BlueLotus: A Reiki Level Two Handbook

Mastering the BlueLotus: A Reiki Master/Teacher Handbook

Any additional projects will be listed on my website as they become available. www.faerywolf.com

www.ingramcontent.com/pod-product-compliance
Lightning Source LLC
Chambersburg PA
CBHW031209090426
42736CB00009B/854